Earth After Rain

Earth After Rain

SHERI BENNING

THISTLEDOWN PRESS

© Sheri Benning, 2001
All rights reserved

No part of this publication may be reproduced or transmitted in any form or by any means, graphic, electronic or mechanical, including photocopying, recording, or any information storage and retrieval system, without permission in writing from the publisher. Requests for photocopying of any part of this book shall be directed in writing to CanCopy, 1 Yonge Street, Suite 1900, Toronto, Ontario, M5E 1E5.

Canadian Cataloguing in Publication Data

Benning, Sheri, 1977 –
Earth after rain

(New leaf editions. Series seven)
ISBN 1-894345-36-3
I. Title. II. Series.
PS8553.E543E27 2001   C811'.6   C2001-911004-9
PR9199.4.B46E27 2001

Book and cover design by J. Forrie
Typeset by Thistledown Press Ltd.
Printed and bound in Canada

Thistledown Press Ltd.
633 Main Street
Saskatoon, Saskatchewan
S7H 0J8

Thistledown Press gratefully acknowledges the financial assistance of the Canada Council for the Arts, the Saskatchewan Arts Board, and the Government of Canada through the Book Publishing Industry Development Program for its publishing program.

ACKNOWLEDGEMENTS

I have deeply benefited from the wisdom of fine teachers such as Tim Lilburn, Hilary Clark and John Livingstone Clark.

Thanks to friends Yuri Corrigan, Miranda Traub, Jenn Still, and Darren Bernhardt, and to the good people at St. Peter's College and Abbey for fostering me and welcoming me into their home.

I am also thankful for the support of the Saskatchewan Writer's Guild, The Saskatchewan Arts Board and everybody at Thistledown Press.

An especial thanks to Kurt, Heather, Rosalie and Larry Benning who, through their daily example, show me that "love is so powerful it makes everything ordinary." (*The Cloud of Unknowing*)

I am grateful to the places these poems visit: the farmscape of St. Peter's Colony, the South Saskatchewan River and Nemeiben Lake, Saskatchewan.

Italicized lines in "Blue Beginning of Flame" are from the poems "Relinquished" and "Paraclete" found in *More Light* by Hilary Clark.

CONTENTS

BONE POLISH	9
WHERE WIND BEGAN	10
IN FLIGHT	12
RUSSIAN THISTLE	13
AN OCEAN I'VE NEVER KNOWN	15
LATE AUGUST MOONWHISPERS TO RIVER	17
HERE, I LEARN NIGHT	18
BEARLETTER/1	20
BEARLETTER/2	21
HEATHER, TONIGHT THE OCEAN	22
WHY I'M AFRAID TO HAVE CHILDREN	23
UNDER THE NOON MOON	25
HE MEANT TO SAY FLOWERS	26
LEARNING MY BODY	28
MORNING	35
BODIES OF STONES	36

YOUR BODY	37
YOUR HANDS	38
DEFINITIONS FROM THE RIVER	39
WATER STILL CONDUCTS US	40
BLIND	42
FIRST SNOW	43
SUDDEN DEPARTURE	45
THE WORLD AS LINES	46
HOW THE NIGHT WAS SPLIT	47
THAT UGLY THING	48
BETWEEN	50
THE WORLD OPEN	51
PLUM TREE ON THE EVE OF LENT	54
THE END OF DEATH	56
IMPOSSIBLE ENDINGS	57
TORN SONG	59
THE BLUE BEGINNING OF FLAME	60

Streak in the eye:
to preserve
a sign borne through the dark,
revived by the sand (or ice?) of
an alien time for a more alien forever
and tuned as a mutely
quivering consonant.

— "Streak" Paul Celan

BONE POLISH

Spit from river, the first canal
my body is land —
belly a pasture for grazing,
feral earth between thighs.

At sunset ravens descend,
ash whirl from dead flame,
a night-mirror black.

They steal me in snatches:
brome hair
dirt flesh.
My eye in a beak,
a river rubbed stone.

A coyote, I am
left to polish my bones
with hunger.

WHERE WIND BEGAN
(to Mary Benning)

September, 1906, a breeze lifted
a salty curl, the colour sparrow
off your Russian white neck.
I can feel that perfect
moment, the slow sky tickle.
It was the first time
Saskatchewan breathed on you.

On the boat to Canada,
you watched mothers
return their dead
children to the first womb.
You saw no division
between sea and night.
Pulled by moon,
curled bodies still
map constellations
mirrored by sky.

Your youngest daughter felt
the heaving Atlantic
as though it was the rise
and fall of a breathing chest.
She gripped life with crabapple fists.

She was the first seed
that rooted you to this land.
You wrapped her in blue

cloth from your wedding dress.
Hypnotic thump of thick soil
on her coffin startled geese,
inspired flight.

Time cannot hide in a space
where everything is open.
I can feel new sky fingering
your sepia curls, its mouth
on your neck,
its graceful
tongue.

IN FLIGHT

Geese rise slow in the dense
of this day. Their wings raise
the weight of damp.

In flight they are responsible
creatures, holding on their backs,
our imperfection.

RUSSIAN THISTLE
(to my father)

I want to tell you about
the russian thistle in the ditch
with flax and clover, dusk's
first stars. How standing
in low sky, a hungry mouth,
sweat buds on my body. Barley
bows beneath shadow, wren-
feathers my legs.

I want to tell you how
the sun behind clouds
is an opal, everything
dusted with motes of
flexing light,

and clouds clenched
with silt-veins are wrinkles
in your brow or crescent
clay-moons beneath your nails
from a lifetime seeding
and harvesting.

I want to tell you
about the russian thistle
in the electric light
of the opal sun, moon

still a frozen whisper.
How a crow-breath
before rain punches
earth releasing
the green of sage
and sap,

the barbs around
its heart remind
me of a beauty
so sharp that
when it enters,
it never leaves.

AN OCEAN I'VE NEVER KNOWN

The last fall
you helped your father
harvest, husks and dust
star-swarmed as you filled
hoppers with currents of seed.
Gathered swaths, a suspended
wake. Chaff in your hair,
yarrow in bootlaces,
you offered me an
arrowhead heated
by your blood.

Your voice
on the phone,
first time in months,
you've moved to the coast.
Until now, fricative wind
and the moon prismed
by dew, its multitude
of reflections electric
on wheat-waves,
is all we knew
of the ocean —

Watching the moon
shatter on the river,

I remember the arrowhead
in your palm like sun-
swallowed coral fossils
found on mountains or
the memory of my body
that you carry on yours,
buried in sounds
of an ocean
I've never
known.

LATE AUGUST MOONWHISPERS TO RIVER

the moon tonight,
a skeletal heart
veined with glyptic
messages, an umber
throb coddled in a nest
of finger laced willows,
a whisper tangled on
the serpent-back river

> *Go deep. Soon*
> *you will be closed*
> *in a cocoon of ice.*
>
> *We will meet in Spring.*
>
> *After chrysalis,*
> *I will be a hidden*
> *mouth on your*
> *surfacing.*

HERE, I LEARN NIGHT
(Nemeiben Lake)

May 3

Setting sun, a throbbing heart contained
by fine cage of rib clouds.
Sun pounds, bruises clouds plum.

      Air I breathe, deer-back coloured.

Loon song — filament stab
threads my ear
pulls me   closer.

May 30

Poplar leaves, weightless moth wings, soak
in fat after supper sun. A grouse assembles
from shadow. Poplar tree, bony colt leg,
stutters in the shocked wake of flight.

I lean against a bear shouldered boulder
my hand, faint web on its hulked lichen back,
pee into thick pubic moss, hunch in ancient
bird remains.

Here I learn night doesn't fall —
it rises from the forest belly.
Night is sky consumed
by jack pine shadow.

May 23

Clouds, a pubis bone,
pull sun inside.

Uterine flex
and sun, newborn head,
is absorbed.

How often has my body done this?
I devour my fecundity. Inside me fireflies,
starry embers spit from flame, muted
by spongy night flesh,

a soundless swallow.

May 31

Dusk sun blurs
boundaries,
leaks amber —

light, a quick tongue in
shuddering poplar leaves,

sun, a pearl of blood
drawn from winter flesh —
                      smeared

BEARLETTER / 1

Bear,

If I continue to walk this path
of sinking light, we will meet.
I am a pale slip of elm-moon
drawn by tides of shadow,
a huffed poplar seed sucked
by lake.

Wood asphodels,
rooted constellations,
guide me.
The forest is thick
with your dank gravity,
a woman-weight
moments before birth.
Sun, a wild rose rotting.
Tendrils of last light tangle
in twigs. Birds flit,
heartbeats — poplar leaf shadows.

I wear your loamy incense:
moss, sloughed
poplar bark,
blue undertones
of moon and rain.

Bear, I don't know how
this will end.

BEARLETTER / 2

Bear,

I have never given birth,
my womb a spring plum,
clenched fist,
sleeping sepaled flower.

But Bear, you teach me birth, your name a verb,
hulked muscles river-roll over your bones
as you hunker. Your holler guttural as
earth tears beneath your paws.

Birthing room, a cave, ice-white walls.
Hibernation over, you hunger-howl.
You are beside   inside
coming out —
          You burrow through a leaf shadow,
emerge from a labium shrouded by
shavegrass, ragweed, passionflower.
Your fur is slick with symbiotic
swamp you left behind. Hunger-howl —
nipples sun-hard chokecherries.

Everywhere your fetid musk:
cracked skin   marsh root
blood   moss   scat

HEATHER, TONIGHT THE OCEAN

Heather, the ocean cleaves us:
a steel wedge we fall from,
a mirror that undresses
differences.

Remember the keen
of the after-dark swing?
Pump, thrust, colt-legs
beat counterpoint.
Moonlit eight year old skin
defines the colour night —
ambiguous pewter.
Our toes above our heads,
pearly stars.

Tonight, the ocean:
a field between magnets.

Always at the end
of your parobola, I watch
you unleash. For a breath
your body divides
earth from sky,
a pale moon
waning.

Tonight, the ocean:
the gut that hurdles us.

WHY I'M AFRAID TO HAVE CHILDREN

Because my bones are doors that enclose you and your arrival will unhinge me. I will dislocate, a tectonic shift.

Because my belly will distend and after I will be a hollow mollusk, streamed with seaweed.

Because your heart is a hummingbird in a nest of filament veins.

Because I might drop you on my scabby linoleum floor as when I dropped my grandma's crystal vase, everywhere prismatic shards.

Because I am 22
                I am 42
                              I am 35. Because l would rather give up my life than my self and you will demand no less.

Because a vampire, who teaches high school during the day, lives in the apartment below my boyfriend's. Late at night little girls file into his lair like animals facing slaughter. When I pass them in the hall, they cover their faces, their hands the colour of yellowing pearls.

Because the pain of your descent hovers like a wasp and my mother who told me I'll forget has been known to lie.

Because the river is veiled by an iridescent skin that conceals a current. Because pregnant women's skin, which is said to glow, conceals what might drown them.

Because your fingertips are wild strawberries, crushable and then sweet bud-blood.

Because I heard that pregnant women in Nazi war camps had their legs tied together and I don't want to know how this could kill me.

Because while sunbathing on a beach last summer I saw a sail, small as your first tooth.

You're like that sail floating on an inland sea. The closer we get, the bigger you become —

UNDER THE NOON MOON

Yesterday at the doctor's,
my x-rayed hips, the cave
we pass through,
what lovers enter into,
what I will look like
after years in earth.

Now under the noon moon,
a shed clover seed, blood-stiff
roseberries and blueberries
with frost-split skins, shards
of speargrass and wind-
crippled goldenrod, sun stirred
by poplars, molasses heat
on my flanneled shoulders —

now under the noon moon,
a deer snort, I stumble
on pelvic-curled driftwood and
remember my bone-glow sifting
dirt. Squall of leaving geese,
thousands of sun-white bellies
jerking on river waves, comforts
me the way a parent does a child
and the child needs no proof.

HE MEANT TO SAY FLOWERS

The doctor said cystitis,
ulcers on bladder.

He meant to say flowers,
wood anemones,

bladder abloom with
pinprick blood globes,

spasms, the opening
of persistent petals.

Inside I am earth after rain,
silty scent escapes from

labia, cave opening
snarled with grass.

Wire roots needle through
my stillness.

The doctor said cystitis,
he meant to shout "Fire!"

My bladder is a bird of fire,
spasms, the opening
of flame-crowned wings.

Dragon breath sears hieroglyphs
in the tunnel of urethra.

Inside I am dark
as the night a forest sheds —

inner thighs, blood burned
birch flesh.

LEARNING MY BODY

> *Each walks not as if on alien soil, but each one's place is its very self, and when it goes on the place where it came from goes with it; it is not one thing itself and its place another.*
> — Plotinus, *Enneads*. V. 8. 3-4

Place hand on the crowned flesh
of a white spruce.

Stare until knuckles are knots,
veins, light in moss.

Stand until hair
steeps sun

                                        Snagged by jackpines,
                                        spiderthread ~

                                        motion suspended
                                        by light.

                                        Sun flexes on my shoulders,
                                        if I move, I will disappear

Rain brings out
the tinct of things ~

licked by its glass eyes, my thighs,
wave-washed shores

                              Rain's slurred syllables
                              hiss into the lake's
                              meniscus ~
                                      roots *bones*
                                                  blood   *skin*
                             sap   *stone*

After a winter in the city, I come to
the forest convinced of my ugliness,

but here, where the horizon is
a serrated line of pine on sky,
the scars on my back are a willow-web

and at the centre of a jackpine,
a lash ~ labial folds parted,
scent of wet flesh.

In the city I ran into winter's lungs
hoping to disappear,
but here, where the lake is
fed by rusting veins,

I run to feel
marsh wind open
my hair ~
       moth wings

eclipse ~
    my index finger on
    a balsam poplar on
    a thistle-tine moon

                      stars ~
                          the afterthought of stone,
                          the light we shuck before
                          we die

birch roots, muscled
fingers, grip stone.

birch body in wind,
a cyle of smoke.

wind loosens roots,
exposes dark beginnings ~

my death is here, too

the forest will
console you ~

wind-felled poplar held
by bare roots

moss after rain ~
    fecund flesh
    of inner
    thigh

            my belly moon-curves
            over knotted pine

            wind-thin fingers
            summon song

loonsong ~
    the reaching sounds
    we make before
    we come

Song is impossible
without the friction
of colliding bodies.
Wind ripens
raven lungs,
dry plums,
kindles a call
that quivers
lake's sky-skin

and raven makes wind
visible, defines the shape
of its body with an oil-
glide, drapes wind
in a soot stained silk

MORNING

and sky is
not severed
from earth —

a lover falls
asleep inside
of you —

fog-swallowed
river

BODIES OF STONES

measure the distance
they've come,
wear river,
and bitter
rain –

in lacunas
of nightbreath
we learn
to hold
each other —

before words
or after

YOUR BODY

Your body reminds me winter is coming.
Outside, elms are consumed with summer's
hungry death. Moon slips through
flitting flames unnoticed.

Your body reaching for me
reminds me winter is coming.
Soon the moon will be held
by elm limbs. Soon
they will be lovers
in crystalline air.

YOUR HANDS

> *nobody, not even the rain has such small hands*
> — e.e. cummings

I'm starting to notice the beauty of small actions. Your hands are a terse verb, cognate of flight. They are white lilies around my silver teapot. Your hands are light encased by a veil of skin. They are the space between words, pause between breath, movement between water and tea. Your hands enjoy the flexible absence of weight. At my approach, your wrists diminish, a fleeting horizon. I hang heavy around you, a miasmic shadow. The teapot rattles, a bag of broken glass. Watch the curving body of rising steam. Your hands are that elusive, fingers, spring-stem slender.

Reflected light announces presence. Your hands,
a subtle affirmation.

DEFINITIONS FROM THE RIVER

Exactitude:
How your voice fits
my ear, stone cut
by water for palm.

Your voice smoke-
curls slow as edges
of sepia photos.

And though I am
a stranger, I feel you
hold my shoulders —
my back a moon
your hand eclipses,
your voice a river lap
my neck a fine fish bone.

I want to come
to you with
   alder
      willow
  poplar —
spring incense
in my hair,
offer you
gathered words,
     gull songs,
definitions
from the river
for your languid
dismantling.

WATER STILL CONDUCTS US

The car leaves a path
of velocity like the tail
of a dying star. We roll
beneath rivulets of aurora borealis
in a sky shouldered by pine.

The lake we leave behind,
a cranial imprint,
ice and snow — strata
of petrified bone,
a closed fontanelle.

Water still conducts us —
love words eddy, the current
that pulls us home.

❧❧❧

Lake under bird-bone ice is a dream,
a bulbous brain. River, a synapse path, bears
intimation of Spring:
                      bud husk homing songs
      auricle confessions of love.
River electric with impulses of thaw.

By a river, I learn corrasion is more communion
than theft. I am shoal you wrap around, lap and recede

with feline gestures. Like river sliding over earth,
your tongue down my belly is left with the taste of silt.

❧❧❧

feathers   shells   petals you gather as you river-travel across day
are neuronic, demand articulation. Your bundles of words, a reflex.
From your bedroom, I listen to you at the computer. Your fingers
speak the cricket voices of rain. Sometimes words escape like your
cat, her body, water enclosed by fur membrane, spilling from your
hands. Sometimes words pour torrentially, necklace snaps, splash of
pearls on fir floor. I fall asleep to the ebb and flow of creation.

❧❧❧

Asleep, I am at the bottom of a lake.
Sleep a season for womb movements,
for assembly of all that we gather, waves upon day.
I wake to feline heat, your body around mine. Night —
room, the colour of a deep bruise, blood-blue slough.
Your breath on my neck, ciliary waves.

Outside, snow falls, soft
as the sound of closing wings,
snowflakes in moonlight,
pointillistic bursts
of pure colour.

At the lake edge, bones thicken.
Fusion, subtle as the pull of night on day,
sudden as a new star on the horizon lip.

BLIND

Through every thing we love, light comes in. Love, an aperture, shows the world in new ways. Intimate knowing prisms, the curve of the ear whispered into when river-silt night lays down on you like sun through rain-sequined sky. The wisest love plurally; they see with compound eyes.

That is why we are disoriented when love leaves. Having lost a way of focus, all sight becomes peripheral.

When my head was on your chest, filled with the ocean sounds of blood, July sky was a bulging vein, air above pavement serpentine as latin dancers. Elm leaves, embossed by the bronze dusk sun, flicked at the moment light's slow tickle became unbearable — tails of jut-ribbed horses. Later we smelled of grass, a lover's lingering scent, hair woven into a shirt.

But now snow falls soft and random, the ohs and ahs of bodies entwined.

Not love, but the absence of,
makes us blind.

FIRST SNOW

i)

Moon tonight, a longing,
a thin wrist through sedge-
clouds, open just enough
to let lost light in.

Dark heat of your hands
around my wrists, thumbs
over star-cold knuckles,
fingers open just enough
to let blood in.

Tomorrow I will wake
to smoke, dying
leaves, streaks
of hair against
my face like elms
outside my window,
arthritic branches
open just enough
to let first snow in.

ii)

Heldbreath blue morning.
Last night's moon,
a humming-
bird wingbone
cloud clamped.

In lily light, we fell
beneath a sieve of elms,
an autumnal heap of
       feathers,   mice skulls,
   shells of words   we didn't mean,
blood sodden leaves —
but today we sleep,

birthed between
hips of snow,
on a belly
of snow,

today
to snow's
slow sough.

SUDDEN DEPARTURE

How you feel
inside me is like
the path of a leaf
falling — the tree, a hand
opening, releasing
thousands of black birds,
frantic punctuation marks,
their wings the absent
flutter of your sleeping lash.

The leaf startled into descent
by sudden departure.

THE WORLD AS LINES

Your paintings, eyes hiss — release of sap
from burning limbs. Shale-shard cheekbones
could draw blood.

In your self-portrait,
cigarette between scissored fingers,
even smoke from your flame-lips slices.

You live autumn alder sharp — choices smoulder
at your feet, shed tooth-leaves. When I come to you,
my heart a soaked poppy, you see my tears as precise,
charted stars.

But it is hard to see the world as lines after realizing night
only dampers day, and water shapes rock
and rock shapes lake.

Hang your self-portrait on waves — watch divisions
bleed, a myopic haze. Lines, butterfly-open,
spill colour.

When clouds are drawn to earth the way lake inhales
poplar down, you will know how it feels to be unsure
if rain rises or falls.

HOW THE NIGHT WAS SPLIT

How the night was split
by stars cat-teeth sharp
and the moon stiff as a swan
feather, how you passed out
at some party and woke to
him on you, a nest of blood,
sweat and hair, his pounding
between your legs reminding
you of waves against the pier
where you sat last october in
pigeon sound and the yellow
smell of death and shit
and how he must have bit
off your tongue, a fish
beached in sun,
because only now
can you tell me —
voice a sparrow-
flight in wind —
of the blood,
the stars,
the night
split.

THAT UGLY THING

My friend in the psych ward
cries unless she's asleep.
Her room dark,
a mouth silenced.

Nurses, bring papercups
of neon-sweet pills
that make her forget
she feels ugly.

Last week, Dad dragged a dead fox
out from under my cabin.
For a day I watched it peripherally,
caught pink glimpses
of its lulled tongue.

When my friend was sixteen
a man tore into her.
And just as wheat sprouts
where a farmer shakes
out his overalls,
a husk split in her womb.

Three months later
she slunk her bloom —
                        blood-sopped petals.

Secrets make a gravity
that pulls on you
until you can't stand —

She told no one.

I want to look at the fox, touch its eyes,
black as what fire leaves behind,
but only a smear remains —
Dad hauled it away, "Didn't want you
to have to look at that ugly thing."

BETWEEN

Nothing just stops. Think of night sucking day, gypsum in the cosmos' humid mouth. Of shadow leaking in halfbreaths from a plum tree. The mountain worn by a feather. How you wake in the morning — then dusk's full-bellied shadows — then sharp stars. You've done nothing but stare and still you couldn't find it. You wish you could taste the space between a beginning and its end, a pomegranate seed, roll it over your tongue, feel concise boundaries, a thin hull, before you bite and swallow —

THE WORLD OPEN

Tears make you believe
you are underwater —
pines seaweed-sway
and the moon wears
the shape of waves.

Mom's heart stops
and all time shifts.
The four hour drive
to the hospital — days.

Our night car travels
the terrain of a cave:
pines —
stalactites,
stars —
bat eyes,
night air —
leather skin.

My fingers through the window
brush wings and I think it's wind.

In the glow of his cigarette, my father's
flesh drips, leaves from november
poplars. Just as bats bring the realization
of night, bodies whorls of breeze,
my father points at death,
its slow smoulder
like the tip of his cigarette
in the cave of my belly.

❦❦❦

Before my brother left to study,
we went to a bar. Despite the pull
of beer on his tongue, he gave us
names for muscles and veins.
We laughed at the feel of latin
on our skin, precise as a microscope,
sounding out each pore.
Without him to translate,
doctor's words hover –
      a cyclone of moths.

Lack of language makes
us involuntary. My sister
holds my hand —

there is only magma-
heat of pounding
blood.

          ※※※

As children we learned tectonic
plates balance on pools of stone.
Tides of heat tore earth apart.
Under winter slate-skies,
my siblings and I drawn
by heat, into our parents'
bed, a web of limbs.

Ears pressed to chests,
we could hear the world
open.

Continents remember Pangea
by the bend in their bodies.
So too, my cheekbone
defines the curve
of mom's hand.

PLUM TREE ON THE EVE OF LENT

blue swells smear
sky, an unlit blood,
a lenten linen.

sky, puffed lung,
aspirates
ashen snow.

dry plum tree
trembles —
an old woman,
moth hands and
arthritic bones
with a crow
on her pewter
shoulder
that croaks:
>*oh hungry lord*
>*oh tired lord*
>*oh lonely, lonely lord*

sky, colour of exhaustion
after a full-body cry, calm
iris of mother eye.

plum tree erect, branches —
brittle spines, sepia crosses

sky, oil pool,
blue crow-coat.

underneath
plum tree branches —
spindly pubic muff

❧❧❧

sky, ash gray granny face —
a slate-soiled veil.

tea-stained plum branches —
knuckled fingers
accuse:
    it was you it was you it was you

THE END OF DEATH
(for Anthony Benning)

This is my body that is for you.
Do this in remembrance of me
              — first letter of Paul to the Corinthians

Earth sucks his body like a seed,
frees him an oiled wood and velvet husk.
Rhizomes bloom in empty eye-nooks.

His body, a loaf of bread broken
by wrung hands of evergreen roots.
They braid leaven-coloured bones.

He transmutes:
blood and flesh feed
fingertip sized nodes

and so his death is
the end of death —

He pulses in flame-
shaped pine cones.

IMPOSSIBLE ENDINGS

Last night
I watched you
lean over your mother.

Vague hospital light
washed you in water-
colour.

Your body's shadow,
stained sedge —
definitions of endings,
impossible.

You told me once
that we all come
from the same DNA —

and in a moment
brief as the clink
of china on stone,

your words
leaf-hover —
we all pass
through the hips

of a familiar
mother.

❧❧❧

At the equinox
they sedate her.

Outside, wheat clenched
by dirt's fists, sates new hunger.

A sharp moon
decrescendos

Earth waits
open.

❧❧❧

The night she dies you lay
your head in the hollow
between my breasts —

heartbeat, careless
wing thrum —

and marvel,
life's smallness —

heartbeat, a sound
you can carry
in a teaspoon.

TORN SONG
(to Yuri)

Standing on the bridge,
your hand on my back,
I want to tell you

how the torn song of gulls
is the sound of the moon
breaking on the river —
waves, obsidian-sharp

how shreds of moon
snared on stippled
waves are wings
taking flight,

how gull wings
in flight are petals
of moon,

how the moon is
a blossom of gull
wing and song —
an unbroken vowel
in sky's throat,

how we are all reeled
into the current
of song.

THE BLUE BEGINNING OF FLAME
(to my late grandmother, Mina Tobin)

i)

alone   hungry   vision wet,
eyes scraped by dust, scales
flayed from the reptilian road.

in the distance heat flickers,
a glass-ghost candescence
over volted-amber canola.

my thoughts flurry,
moths muttering
minaminamina

ii)

the soul finds solace
where it can —
standing in canola
everything is focused
by sky, blue irises
of her eyes,

moon,
a gull-feather falling
barn,
a blood blister
my heart
pulsing her name
                    Mina

iii)

I lie on a gull-glyph pocked beach,
sand, withered bone,
bodies, sunned-stones.

A child plays near me,
eyes the colour of tiger-
lily stamens.

the spirit speaks
from the flame
throats of flowers —

My face twice seized
in the opalesce of eyes, I see
how I looked when she held
my head in her hands.

iv)

Once, while painting, she
told me to remember skies,
not clouds, are blue —
tip of her brush stained
the blue beginning
of flame.

Cradled by the beach,
a forearm with cilial hair
blonding in sun, watching
a thunderstorm bloom,

I remember —
white clouds,
flesh that fell from her
reaching arm,

blue sky,
quill-veins
on the back
of her palm.

She germinates
in me a desire
for clarity.

v)

death shoves, whiteknuckles
its way out of the ground —
Free from petal-curled
flesh, gull-white bones
are letters.

Now she is
a lexis that de-
composes poems.

vi)

In the city, a man asks if he can bum a smoke.
His fingers wicks, nails burnt pollen-umber.

Now, near the beach,
tiger lilies would be
monarch wings steeped
in rain. Petals, nicotine
stained, curling like hair
at her nape.

Spring pleads perpetually
out of the throats
of the dying —

The man touches me
with candelabra hands.
Day winnows away,
there are only
finger-flames,
aureoles
around
her face —
                      would it be would it be

AGMV Marquis
MEMBER OF SCABRINI MEDIA
Quebec, Canada
2001